MY ZONE

MY ZONE

ANIMAL RESCUE

ANITA GANERI

EDGE
W
FRANKLIN WATTS

LONDON•SYDNEY

**FIRST PUBLISHED IN 2010 BY
FRANKLIN WATTS
338 EUSTON ROAD
LONDON NW1 3BH**

FRANKLIN WATTS AUSTRALIA
LEVEL 17/207 KENT STREET
SYDNEY NSW 2000

SERIES EDITOR: ADRIAN COLE
ART DIRECTOR: JONATHAN HAIR
DESIGN: BLUE PAW DESIGN
PICTURE RESEARCH: DIANA MORRIS
CONSULTANT: FIONA M. COLLINS,
     ROEHAMPTON UNIVERSITY

A CIP CATALOGUE RECORD OF THIS BOOK
IS AVAILABLE FROM THE BRITISH LIBRARY

ISBN: 978 0 7496 9571 2

DEWEY CLASSIFICATION: 636'.0832

ACKNOWLEDGEMENTS:
Adrio Communications/Shutterstock: 31. Courtesy of Africat/www.
africat.org: 32-33. Hintan Aliakel/Shutterstock: 9t. Baxternator/
istockphoto: 7b. www.beautynaturals.co.uk: 36t. Brendan Beirne/
Rex Features: 21. M Booth/IFAW: 23t, 23b. Brasil2/istockphoto:
26. CC: 29c. Konstantin Chagrin/Shutterstock: 17. C.H.A.T./
www.celiahammond.org: 20. CostinT/istockphoto: 7t. Dino4/
istockphoto: 28t. Damion Diplock/RSPCA PL: 14. EcoPrint/
Shutterstock:18-19. Andrew Forsyth/RSPCA PL: 15b, 16t, 16b.
49pauly/istockphoto: 43c. Four Oaks/Shutterstock: 25b. Michael
Friedel/Rex Features: 27c. Garo/Phanie/Rex Features: 34. Eric
Gevaert/Shutterstock: 41t. Eileen Groome/istockphoto: 13. Den
Guy/istockphoto: 43ca. Mark Hatfield/istockphoto: 43t. Hedrus/
Shutterstock: 30t. Christoph Henning/Das/Alamy: 36b. Loretta
Hostettler/istockphoto: 6. Ingret/Shutterstock: 8t. Eric Isselée/
istockphoto: 8b. Eric Isselée/Shutterstock: 9b, 24b, 44. Marcel
Jancovic/Shutterstock: 43b. Ray Johnson/Alamy: 39. Warwick
Lister-Kaye/istockphoto: 43cb. Lucy McCarthy /RSPCA PL: 16c.
Hannah Morris/Shutterstock: 4, 5. Becky Murray/RSPCA PL: 15t.
Nowzad Dogs/www.nowzaddogs.co.uk: 22. Howard Oates/
istockphoto: 25t. www.peta.org: 35. Photoresearchers/SPL: 28b.
Photoshot Holdings/Alamy: 40. Graeme Purdy/istockphoto:
30b. Quavondel/istockphoto: 24t. Rex Features: 11b, 37. Debra
L Rothenburg/Rex Features: 11t. RSPCA PL: 12. SasPartout/
istockphoto: front cover. Debbi Smirnoff/istockphoto: 41b. Charles
H Smith/U.S. Fish & Wildlife Service: 29t. WENN: 10. Lisa Maree
Williams/Getty Images: 38. A S Zain/Shutterstock: 40c. Zilli/
istockphoto: 7c. ZSL PL: 29b.

EVERY ATTEMPT HAS BEEN MADE TO CLEAR COPYRIGHT.
SHOULD THEIR BE ANY INADVERTENT OMISSION PLEASE
APPLY TO THE PUBLISHER FOR RETIFICATION

PRINTED IN CHINA

FRANKLIN WATTS IS A DIVISION OF
HACHETTE CHILDREN'S BOOKS,
AN HACHETTE UK COMPANY.
WWW.HACHETTE.CO.UK

Please note: every effort has been made by the Publishers
to ensure that the websites in this book contain no
inappropriate or offensive material. However, because of the
nature of the Internet, it is impossible to guarantee that the
contents of these sites will not be altered. We strongly advise
that Internet access is supervised by a responsible adult.

LOOK OUT FOR...

Words highlighted in the text can be found in the glossary.

ANIMAL RESCUE? WHAT'S THAT?

Animal rescue only happens when an animal is in trouble. This can be for lots of different reasons. Most people look after their pets well, but some do not. Some wild animals need rescuing, too. Perhaps they are being hunted.

Vets, like this one, play a big part in helping animals that have been rescued.

WEBtag

You will see WEBtags throughout this book. Many websites feature more information about the articles inside, videos and up-to-date news and blogs.

Pets are animals that need our love, protection and care. We are **responsible** for them, which means they need us for everything, from food to shelter. But other animals, like this tiger cub, also need our help.

Inside you will find lots of pet advice and stories from around the world – from zoos to rescue centres. Plus there are lots of views to think about and to chat about with your friends.

I'm a lorikeet at Lowry Park Zoo, Tampa, USA.

TOP TEN PETS

Are you planning to get your first pet friend, but can't decide which is the best? Here's a **MY ZONE** guide to ten of the most popular pets.

1 Cat Cats are the most popular pets on the planet, with more than 600 million worldwide.

2 Dog There are more than 400 **breeds** of dog, from teeny Chihuahuas to gigantic Great Danes.

3 Bird A pet budgie in England can recite a whole Chinese takeaway menu. Cheep! Cheep!

4 Fish Goldfish were first kept as pets in China 4,500 years ago – they're still popular today.

5 Rabbit Keep two or more rabbits together. These sociable creatures don't like living on their own.

6 Hamster

A dwarf Russian hamster is only 5 cm long, small enough to fit on your little finger.

7 Tortoise

Tortoises can live for 100 years, so you will have this pet for your whole life. (Some countries have banned people from keeping them.)

8 Lizard

Lizards, such as geckos, need special lighting, heating and food that may include live insects.

9 Stick Insect

Wild stick insects can grow to over 30 cm long. Luckily, pet stick insects are much, much shorter.

10 Pony

People first used horses for riding about 5,000 years ago. A pony is a small horse.

http://www.allaboutpets.org.uk/home.aspx

WEBtag The Blue Cross expert site, featuring fact sheets and news features.

STAR PETS

Your pet is supposed to say a lot about who you are. Here's the low down on some star pets – you'll have to make up your own mind about their owners!

Cheryl Cole owns a cheeky Chihuahua called Buster. He digs holes in her garden and buries her clothes. He's also been blamed for making Cheryl late for stage appearances – by snarling at her when she tries to leave. Buster also peed on the *X Factor* studio carpet.

WEBtag Find out how you can become a responsible dog owner.

http://www.akc.org/public_education/responsible_dog_owner.cfm

Paris Hilton is often seen carrying Tinkerbell, her pet Chihuahua. In 2004, Tinkerbell went missing from Paris's house, but was found later. Paris Hilton has been voted worst celebrity dog owner in an online poll for her poor dog-parenting skills.

US President Barack Obama and his wife chose a black-and-white Portuguese Water Dog, called Bo, to live with them at the White House. The breed is a good one to choose for children who have **allergies**.

http://obama-dog.com

WEBtag Bo's dog blog, complete with photos and expert advice.

11

IS HAVING A PET OK?

Are you already a pet owner? Millions of people are. They love and look after their pets, and wouldn't be without them. But not all pets are so pampered. Many are badly neglected, cruelly treated or simply abandoned (left alone).

So, is having a pet ever okay?

WEBtag Hard-hitting website featuring some shocking videos. (You have been warned!)

http://www.peta.org

NO!

- Keeping animals such as birds and rabbits in cages and hutches is cruel.
- About 1,000 unwanted dogs are **put to sleep** every week .
- Some people kill their pets simply by not feeding them. The dogs in this photo were found in a back garden.

WEBtag Click on 'pet care advice' for the latest care leaflets.

http://www.petcare.org.uk

Be a purr-fect pet owner

If you're thinking of getting a pet, ask yourself these questions first:

1 Can you give it a good home?

2 Can you spend time with it?

3 Can you give it enough exercise?

4 Can you afford its food and vet's bills?

5 Can you make sure it's looked after when you're away?

6 Can you look after it for the rest of its life?

If the answer to any of these is NO, think again. If the answer to all of these is YES, you could be the purr-fect pet owner.

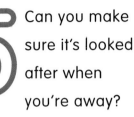

YES!

o Pet owners love and care for their pets. Their pets can become their best friends.

o Pet owners are happier and healthier than people who don't have pets.

o Having a pet teaches you to look after another living thing.

MY RESCUE PET

Thousands of unwanted pets end up in animal rescue centres where they're looked after until they find new homes. So if you're thinking of getting a new pet, why not pop along...

Pet adoption guide

If you're planning to **adopt** an animal, here's what to do:

1. Visit your local animal rescue centre and talk to someone who works there.

2. Meet the animals to find the right pet for you.

DID YOU KNOW?
Every year between 5–7 million animals enter rescue centres in the USA. Less than 2% of 'lost and found' cats are returned to their owners (usually because they were microchipped or wearing a tag).

WEBtag Check out the videos and diaries at this site from IAS.

http://www.internationalanimalrescue.org/

3. A worker visits your home to check it is pet friendly.
4. Take your new pet home. (You pay a small fee for microchipping, **neutering/spaying** and **vaccination**.)
5. Later, a worker calls you to check how your pet is settling in.

If you can't have a pet, why not sponsor one instead? For a few pounds a month, you'll get a photo, certificate, news updates, and you can visit whenever you like. Your donation will pay for food, vet's bills and day-to-day care.

AT THE DOG RACES

Greyhound racing is a multi-million pound industry. If a greyhound stays healthy and injury-free, it can have a career of about three years. But the stress of training and racing can be tough.

These greyhounds race about once a week. But some trainers use drugs to force them to work harder.

Some people argue for greyhound racing, saying it is fun for people to watch and the dogs love to run. Others argue that it should be stopped. Greyhounds cannot go on racing after they are 4 years old, but they can live until they are 14. After their racing careers are over, many are put to sleep or simply abandoned. The lucky ones end up in greyhound rescue centres. So, how do you feel about greyhound racing? Is it entertainment – or **exploitation**?

Greyhounds run around an oval dirt track. They are trained to chase a pretend hare to the finish line.

http://www.iams.com

WEBtag Iams website featuring a greyhound guide. Click Support/ Breed Guide.

GREYHOUND RESCUE

Wags Greyhound Rescue was started by Holly Foster in 1987. She was angry that so many greyhounds were being poorly treated after their racing days were over.

Now Wags has three full-time staff, including Deb (see right). They care for the greyhounds while they try to find them loving homes. Wags is an animal charity – one of hundreds in the UK – and survives on donations from the public.

In Ancient Egypt, greyhounds were prized pets and hunting dogs. Anyone found guilty of killing a greyhound was put to death.

1. When Max came to Wags, he was very scared.
2. The staff at Wags gave Max lots of love and care, and soon he was feeling better.
3. There are thousands of other greyhounds out there who face an uncertain future when they stop racing.

Monday – There are 50 greyhounds in the rescue so there's plenty to do. They've all had breakfast so it's time for a walk. Then I'll clean out their kennels. Lucky me!

Tuesday – I'm off to fetch two stray greyhounds that have been found alone on the street. They're thin and very frightened. But I bet they're gorgeous.

Wednesday – I gave Miley and Zac (the two strays) a good bath this morning. Then I took them to the vet's for a check up. They behaved themselves brilliantly.

Thursday – My day off! I took my two dogs (greyhounds, of course) for a walk and told them how lucky they are.

Friday – A family came to choose a dog. They really liked Miley and Zac. They're coming back at the weekend. Fingers crossed!

PUPPY FARMS

A puppy farm might sound like a pleasant place where cute little puppies run happily in the fields. Except that puppy farms are NOTHING like that at all.

WEBtag The Celia Hammond Trust website features lots of animal rescue stories (contains distressing images).

http://www.celiahammond.org

Puppy farms are places that breed dogs in large numbers for profit. The dogs are often kept in tiny, dirty cages, with little food and exercise. Bitches (female dogs) may be stressed and worn-out from having litter after litter of pups.

Many of the puppies bought from puppy farms have life-threatening illnesses, such as parvo virus and pneumonia, and may die within a few weeks.

So, if you're thinking of buying a puppy...

o Always see the puppy with its mother in the place where the puppy was born. These puppies are in a shop window – which is banned in many countries.

o Check that the puppy has been vaccinated and has a vaccination card.

o Find out as much about the breeder as possible.

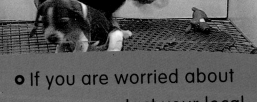

o If you are worried about a puppy, contact your local welfare organisation.

o Join a campaign to put an end to puppy farming (it's also called puppy trafficking).

HAPPY TAILS

Don't miss these amazing tales of real-life rescues, and their happy endings!

DOG OF WAR

When British Royal Marine, Pen Farthing, rescued Nowzad in 2006, this brave hound was in a terrible state. He'd been used for dog-fighting in war-torn Afghanistan. Pen gave him food, shelter and kindness, but when Pen returned home, Nowzad's future looked bleak.

Luckily, Pen found him a place in a rescue centre in Afghanistan. Unluckily, it was a two-day car journey through dangerous territory. Did Nowzad survive? Yes, he did! Once he was better, he was sent to the UK and now lives with Pen.

http://www.nowzaddogs.co.uk

WEBtag Photos, news and videos from the team that rescued Nowzad.

STRANDED KITTY

In October 2009, a devastating typhoon struck the Philippines. Thousands of people fled for their lives. But people weren't the only victims. Thousands of animals also faced drowning and starving to death.

WEBtag Catch up with the latest IFAW news, photos and videos on the rescue blogs.

http://www.ifaw.org

A team of emergency relief rapid responders from IFAW (International Fund for Animal **Welfare**) raced to the scene. Over the next two weeks, they helped more than 3,000 animals. These included a terrified tabby kitten stranded on a hot, metal roof without any water or food.

ASK A VET

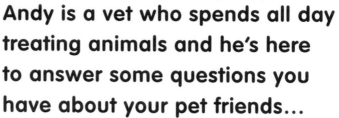

Andy is a vet who spends all day treating animals and he's here to answer some questions you have about your pet friends...

Q

I live in a high-rise flat. Is it okay to have a cat?

Andy says: Most cats like to go outdoors and won't enjoy being cooped up inside. But if the cat doesn't show any signs of being unhappy and has enough space, it should be okay. You will need to provide it with a litter tray in a quiet place.

Q

Why does my dog howl when I go out?

Andy says: Your dog probably has something called separation anxiety. That means it is frightened of being left alone. Help your dog get used to it by leaving him for short periods at first, then gradually increase the time. Don't leave your dog for more than four hours.

Q Is it okay to keep a goldfish in a goldfish bowl?

Andy says: It depends on the size of the bowl! If the bowl is too small, there won't be enough oxygen in the water for your fish to breathe. A large aquarium is best. Put in plenty of water plants to provide oxygen and cover, and some rocks for hiding places.

Q What should I do if I find a baby bird?

Andy says: The best thing to do is to leave it alone. Its nest is likely to be nearby and its parents will take care of it. If you're worried about it being attacked by cats, put it safely on a ledge. If you think a bird is injured, put it in a dark, warm box and take it to the vet.

Q What should I do if I see someone being cruel to an animal?

Andy says: Phone an animal welfare organisation, such as the RSPCA in England or the ASPCA in the USA. They have 24-hour helplines. You'll need to be able to describe the animal and where you saw it.

GOING, GOING...

Pets aren't the only animals in trouble. All over the world, wild animals are dying. Thousands of species of animals are endangered. This means that there are so few of them left that they could disappear altogether and become extinct – gone forever.

WHY ARE ANIMALS IN DANGER?

○ Animal **habitats** are being destroyed (like the forest in this photograph). Some are burned to create new farmland. Animals are left with nowhere to live and no food to eat.

Species of animals have always died out naturally. That's what happened to the dinosaurs millions of years ago. But scientists believe that animals are now becoming extinct 10,000 times faster because of things human beings are doing to the world.

This baby owl has been taken from the wild for the pet trade.

o People have introduced species, such as rats, that eat existing animal eggs and plants, causing them to die out.

o **Climate change** is making the world warmer and creatures are struggling. Tree frogs, for example, die if they become too hot.

o Animals are still being taken from the wild for the pet trade, which breaks an international agreement called CITES. See WEBtag above.

o Some rare animals are being killed for their meat, skins, tusks and other body parts.

o Wildlife is being poisoned by chemicals washed into rivers and the sea from farms and factories.

...GONE!

For these five unfortunate animals, it's too late. They are already extinct.

1 DODO

Once found in: Mauritius
Last one seen: 1680s
Extinct because: hunted for their meat; eggs eaten by cats, dogs and pigs brought to the island.

2 QUAGGA

Once found in: South Africa
Last one seen: 1883
Extinct because: hunted for their meat and hides, and to clear grazing land for livestock.

3 GOLDEN TOAD

Once found in: Costa Rica
Last seen: 1989
Extinct because: pools dried up in unusually warm weather so tadpoles died.

4 YANGTZE RIVER DOLPHIN

Once found in: Yangtze River, China
Last one seen: 1997
Extinct because: river pollution, collisions with boats and fishing nets.

WEBtag Check out the videos and photo galleries at this site.

http://www.edgeofexistence.org

5 CASPIAN TIGER

Once found in: Central Asia
Last one seen: 1970s
Extinct because: killed so habitat could be cleared for farmland.

BIG CAT CARE

The AfriCat Foundation in Namibia was started in 1991 to look after endangered big cats, such as cheetahs and leopards. It rescues big cats, looks after them, then releases most of them back into the wild.

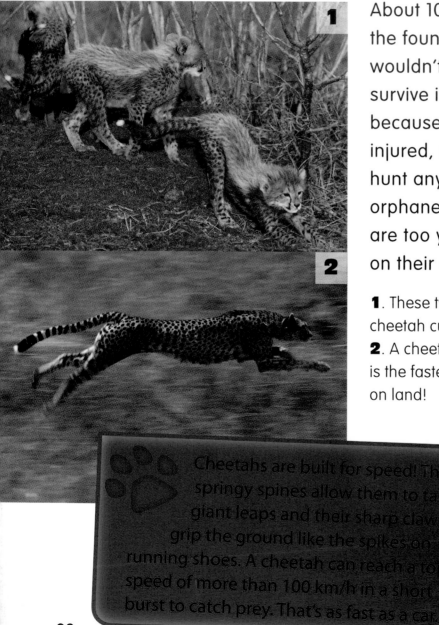

About 100 cats live at the foundation. They wouldn't be able to survive in the wild because they are injured, unable to hunt any more or are orphaned babies who are too young to cope on their own.

1. These two young cheetah cubs are orphans.
2. A cheetah at full speed is the fastest mammal on land!

Cheetahs are built for speed! Their springy spines allow them to take giant leaps and their sharp claws grip the ground like the spikes on running shoes. A cheetah can reach a top speed of more than 100 km/h in a short burst to catch prey. That's as fast as a car.

Cheetah Fact File

Found in: Mostly southern and eastern Africa.

Habitat: They live in grasslands, among the tall grass and bushes.

Fur: Adult cheetahs have golden-brown fur with round, black spots and black rings on their tails. Babies have grey fur with fluffy manes to help camouflage them among the grass.

Size: Adult cheetahs grow about 150 cm long, with another 80 cm of tail.

Diet: They feed mainly on small antelopes, such as gazelles, springbok and impala. They also eat young warthogs, birds and rabbits.

Rare: They are classified as 'endangered' because their habitat is being destroyed and taken over by humans. Plus, farmers kill them because the cheetahs kill livestock. Young cheetahs are also captured for the pet trade.

Dave is a ranger at AfriCat. A call has just come through that there is a cheetah in trouble. Let's join him on a real-life cheetah rescue.

1. The rangers get a call that a wild cheetah has been caught in a farmer's trap. It has been there for several days.
2. They load up the jeep and set off. Once there, Dave checks the cheetah. It is scared but unharmed. He loads his **tranquiliser dart** gun.

3. Dave fires a tranquiliser dart. In a few minutes, the cheetah is fast asleep.
4. While the cheetah snoozes, Dave examines it for any signs of injury or illness. Then the rangers load it into a crate on the jeep and head back to the foundation.

5. The still-sleepy cheetah is weighed and measured.

6. Carla microchips the cheetah so the rangers can keep track of its future movements.

7. About 24 hours later, the cheetah is loaded back into the jeep and driven to a new area, away from any farmland. Then the rangers set it free. Another successful rescue!

5

6

7

WEBtag Find out more about Africat, the big cat rescue organisation.

http://www.africat.org

ANIMAL EXPERIMENTS

Each year, millions of animals are used in lab experiments. These experiments test the safety of new medicines and products, such as household cleaners.

How do you feel about animal experiments?

FOR...

"Without being able to test new drugs on animals, we wouldn't be able to decide which ones are safe to give to humans. That means it would be harder to find drugs to help cure diseases, such as cancer, one of the biggest killers of humans. So the benefits to people outweigh any suffering to the animals."

http://www.understanding
animalresearch.org.uk

WEBtag Website that addresses questions about animal testing.

AGAINST...

"Causing animals to suffer can never be right. Besides, the tests are not always reliable and drugs that work in animals may still not work in humans. And there's no need to test products on animals. There's also the way animals are kept in labs – in cramped conditions."

NUMBER OF EXPERIMENTS ON ANIMALS IN THE UK IN 2008:

Mice: 2,418,604
Rats: 355,370
Guinea pigs: 29,293
Hamsters: 3,298
Gerbils: 1,092
Other rodents: 866
Rabbits: 17,060
Cats: 360
Dogs: 6,105
Ferrets: 1,122
Other carnivores: 1,264
Horses/Donkeys: 89,365
Pigs: 6,824
Goats: 499
Sheep: 35,820
Cattle: 2,302
Deer: 63
Birds: 123,259
Reptiles: 109
Amphibians: 32,674
Fish: 605,155
Marmoset/Tamarin Monkeys: 368
Macaque Monkeys: 4,230
Other mammals: 978
GM animals (genetically modified by humans in a lab): 1,335,560

This monkey is strapped to a metal frame while tests are carried out.

http://www.buav.org

WEBtag Features investigations, news and campaigns about animal testing (contains distressing images).

35

ARE ZOOS COOL OR CRUEL?

Some people believe all animals should be free to live in the wild, and not in zoos. Others believe that zoos help to promote animal welfare and understanding. What do you think?

COOL ZOOS

o Have full-time keepers and really look after their animals' welfare.

o Educate people and allow them to see animals they wouldn't see otherwise.

o Design enclosures to be as close to an animal's natural habitat as possible.

o Breed endangered animals, then release them into the wild.

o Do valuable research behind the scenes into animal behaviour and lifestyles to help protect them.

WEBtag Website of one of the world's top zoos – including pages on Terri Irwin (above).

http://www.australiazoo.com.au

CRUEL ZOOS

○ Don't care for their animals and are only interested in making money from them.

○ Keep the animals in small cages and enclosures, nothing like their natural homes.

○ Don't feed the animals properly or give them enough to do.

○ Don't stop people feeding the animals, or pestering them.

○ Release zoo-bred animals into the wild where they don't know how to survive.

 This Siamang ape is in a zoo cage in Indonesia.

http://www.captiveanimals.org

WEBtag Features lots of news, facts and videos from CAPS about zoos and circuses.

TO THE RESCUE!

FOCUS ON:

Borneo Orang-utan Survival (BOS)

Set up in 1999, BOS is the world's biggest ape rescue centre and is home to more than 600 orang-utans. The orang-utans stay at the centre for at least five years before they can be released back into the wild.

Orang-utans are seriously endangered and around 5,000 are dying or being killed every year. If nothing is done to save them, they'll be extinct in 10 years' time.

http://www.savethe
orangutan.org

WEBtag Website of BOS, featuring news and links to international websites.

Some are adult orang-utans who have been left homeless because their rainforest habitat has been cut down. (You can see patches of cleared forest below.) Others are orphaned babies rescued from the illegal pet trade.

FOCUS ON: The Black Dog Rescue Project

The Black Dog Rescue Project was set up in 2009 to look after abandoned or neglected black dogs in Utah, USA.

Strangely, black dogs are often the last to be adopted from animal rescue centres. Nobody really knows why. The project aims to find new homes for these pooches and to stop dog dumping.

http://www.blackdogrescueproject.com

WEBtag Includes dog training tips and rescue stories.

WORKING WITH ANIMALS

Would you like to work with animals? Here are some suggestions to get you started.

1 VET

Qualifications: A university degree in veterinary science.

Job details: Working with pets, farm or wild animals, treating them and performing surgery. Some vets work in animal hospitals or for animal rescue centres.

2 VET NURSE

Qualifications: College course and work experience.

Job details: Providing expert nursing care for sick animals, supervised by a vet. You'll help look after animals before, after and during operations and treatments.

3 ANIMAL INSPECTOR

Qualifications: Training course. You'll need to be fit, able to drive and good with people.

Job details: Investigating complaints of cruelty, carrying out rescues and inspecting pet shops, farms etc. You'll also give advice about caring for animals.

4 ANIMAL RANGER

Qualifications: Training course and work experience.

Job details: Looking after animals in zoos and wildlife parks. You'll be responsible for feeding the animals, making sure they're healthy and cleaning out their enclosures.

5 DOG TRAINER

Qualifications: Training courses. You'll also need to be good with people…and dogs.

Job details: Training pet dogs and guide dogs for the blind. You'll run training classes and also work with owners and their pets on a one-to-one basis.

GLOSSARY

Adopt – take on an animal as a pet, often from an animal charity or rescue centre.

Allergies – reactions like sneezing, coughing or having itchy skin. Some people get these when they are close to an animal's fur.

Breeds – different types of dog and other animals.

Climate change – the way in which the Earth's climate is changing because of things that human beings are doing.

Donations – gifts of money, often given to charities.

Endangered – animals that are in danger of dying out forever.

Exploitation – taking advantage of an animal in a bad way.

Extinct – animals that have died out forever.

Habitats – the types of places where animals live in the wild.

Microchipped – when a tiny electronic chip is put under an animal's skin. Each chip has a code that can be used to identify the animal if it gets lost.

Neglected – not given proper care, food, water or shelter.

Neutering – when an animal has its reproductive parts removed so that it cannot have babies.

Put to sleep – when an old or sick animal is given an injection that causes it to die.

Responsible – being in charge of an animal's life and care.

Spaying – when the reproductive parts are removed from a female animal so she cannot have babies.

Species – animals that are grouped together because they have similar features.

Sponsor – to give money to an animal rescue centre or charity to look after an animal.

Tranquiliser dart – a dart fired from a rifle that sticks in an animal's skin and makes it sleepy.

Vaccination – an injection that protects an animal from various diseases.

Welfare – in this sense, the wellbeing (happiness, health and safety) of animals.

MORE WEBSITES

http://www.cats.org.uk/learn
Downloadable information and activity packs from
Cats Protection.

http://www.lowryparkzoo.com
Download free animal information podcasts from this
Lowry Park Zoo website.

http://www.bbc.co.uk/cbbc/wild/working
Find out more about working with animals on this BBC
website, which includes photostories.

http://www.rspca.org.uk
Click on the 'media' tab for links to the RSPCA video
library. Also, click on the 'teachers' tab for factsheets,
photos and other curriculum-linked resources.

http://www.wwf.org
Global portal for the WWF - click on WWF International
where you'll find tiger videos and photos.

**http://www.bbc.co.uk/nature/
programmes/tv/a_hospital**
An old website from the Animal
Hospital TV series, but it still
features videos of behind-the-
scenes at an animal rescue
centre. It also has links to
pet fact files.

INDEX